BEING OWNED

A DECADE IN PROFESSIONAL DECLUTTERING

JASMINE SLEIGH

Cover art by: Sameera Ayub, 99Designs
Cover photo by: Matt Austin
Book design by: SWATT Books Ltd

Printed in the United Kingdom
First Printing, 2023

ISBN: 978-1-7392826-0-8 (Paperback)
ISBN: 978-1-7392826-1-5 (eBook)

Jasmine Sleigh
Exmouth, Devon

www.changeyourspace.co.uk

CONTENTS

JASMINE SLEIGH

INTRODUCTION
TEN YEARS IN CUPBOARDS

I have spent ten years in other people's cupboards. A thousand homes, millions of belongings, and all those people reacting in their own way to their stuff. The recent ten-year anniversary of running my own professional decluttering business has left me reflecting on the highs and lows, amazing poignant tales, and frightening flashbacks. There have been some strange and wonderful things and unusual but touching encounters as I have stood as the mediator between owner and their encroaching stockpile.

It is a peculiar job being a professional declutterer. For start, I am not sure I like the title as I do not tend to use the word 'clutter'. This is due to years of being constantly surprised by what people will consider valuable and untouchable, and what others will call rubbish. There is then the uncertainty of its status, where no one seems to know if it is more of a trade or a therapeutic intervention. Clients have an expectation of a finished result that relies on your eye for detail, experience, and skill in that field. Instagram accounts from declutterers are full of time-lapse tidying-up montages that present the amazing before and after of a room as if the client was not present. Yet my experience is that the most important service they will be provided with is the gradual coaching in taking back control, making decisions, and steering the course of changing their space to suit their needs. Perhaps it is closer to being a personal trainer for excess stuff. We are there to challenge, support changing habits, praise progress and be alongside the hard work of slimming down the volume in homes.

These ten years of decluttering led me to reflect on what I bring to the job as a person. I was raised in council housing in a single parent family where money was tight, and it was important to make the most of what we had. Those formative years shaped my thinking about striving for opportunities rather than being concerned with what we had materially. I completed a degree in Psychology and Counselling, post-graduate Certificate in Leadership and Change, and had a successful career in local government. I met a lovely chap, got married, had a baby who has now grown to be a teenager. Then I set up my own business, 'Change Your Space', offering a service no-one had really heard of in Devon at that point.

The first five years I was all alone in my decluttering venture until I met Rachel who has become a key ally. We met as we walked our children on the same route to school and found we were ideologically similar regarding recycling and reuse, and we are both unafraid of hard work. We have been sorting homes together ever since, and, though they do not say it, I am sure many of the clients prefer Rachel to me. That is fine, as I know we are there because we make a good team.

This book is an effort to unpack some of the larger themes that make the work occasionally amazing and sometimes unwieldy, but always poignant. The stories in this book are real, though names have been changed and narratives merged, and some specific details altered to maintain confidentiality. I have arranged them to show a truthful essence of what I have seen in my work being in cupboards, focusing not on the strange artifacts we have found, but the curious interplay with the contents of our homes. It may make you reflect upon your own relationship with your possessions, and if it does, that is great and may be the reason you were drawn to this book. You can perhaps be reassured that you are not alone in feeling conflicted about letting stuff go.

In the trade we say that it is "rarely about the stuff". What we are up against are the entrenched coping mechanisms or self-soothing techniques that the client may be unaware of and have been operating under for many years. I can stand in the mire of seemingly useless stuff that is hindering them and putting them at risk, and we know it is a manifestation of their inner world. It can be desperately sad to see the tree rings of the unravelling of dignity and care as we make our way through the layers of a hoard. You literally feel the weight and restriction of it as we lift and carry and twist to find footing and ways through.

The most common question I am asked is, "What is the worst job you have ever been to?" I find this an awkward question to answer, for several reasons. Firstly, the service is personal and confidential, and I do not like to spill out about what happens in case anyone thinks I would discuss their home as gleeful shock gossip. Secondly, as many other professions will attest, there is a useful barrier that is built up to compartmentalise work that may be unpleasant to recall outside of working hours. Thirdly, the sorts of answers that I think people are looking for are the unusual homes with unexpected collections, or the grim conditions of some homes that can make us feel better as we know our homes are "not as bad as that".

The homes have only occasionally resembled those on extreme hoarding television programmes. Work is more commonly conducted in an average home under pressure with someone who does not know where to begin. They use words like "stuck" and "overwhelmed" to describe the atrophy and stress that an overload of belongings can bring. Some homes though have been shockingly full, and any normal life has been squeezed out.

Sure, we have worked in a small house that had over seventy life-sized mannequins that were not to be moved, and a third floor flat that had over a hundred large electric appliances that did have to come out, and we have also unpacked twenty massive dog ornaments into a small retirement apartment. We have also worked around faeces, found machetes, Third Reich themed memorabilia, unusual sex toys, and we have dug into sort out belongings knowing there was a lost corn snake on the loose in the home somewhere.

However, from my perspective, the worst homes are those where you return a week later to find they have been filled up even further than before, or their worry about their belongings makes them defensive and angry with the person touching them, so the decluttering team are in the firing line. The tough jobs then are when we can see that anxiety and fear are winning and are making the client want to build a psychological wall (or even a physical one of more stuff) perhaps even higher than before, to keep us and the world out. With my own eyes I have seen a mountain of stuff actively impoverish a person's life.

There are tales of hope and we have helped homes to be reclaimed from being previously buried under stuff, and donated hundreds of tons of clothing, shoes, books, ornaments, crafting items, toys, games and furniture to charitable causes. The transformations can be extraordinary. Whole rooms, carpets and furniture seen properly for the first time in years. We have protected many tenancies and opened opportunities for vulnerable people to stay living in their own homes and access personal care. Heating has been able to be reconnected, and people able to sit once more in an armchair and sleep in a bed which had previously been unavailable to them due to a wall of their belongings. It is a source of continued purpose in our vocation that lost and treasured belongings are rediscovered, and that our work has been life-changing.

I wished to simply observe common themes emerging from decluttering with clients and wanted to share their stories for you to reflect on what you take from their experience. So, with ten years alongside people where belongings lay bare the struggles of their inner world, I am asking, who is winning? The stuff or us? Or is it not a combative relationship but one which both sides have something to gain? Let's find out...

JASMINE SLEIGH

DARREN
FREE TO PLAY

It was a bright sunny morning in May as I walked up the garden path to visit Darren's home. He was a tall, bearded gentleman in baggy clothes and wore an apologetic look as he fumbled for his keys. On unlocking the front door, he found it would not budge to open sufficiently for us to enter. With his permission, I managed to squeeze in sideways and shut myself in and there I was able to upright a heavy memory foam mattress that was pressed against the door so we could open it sufficiently to make our way inside.

Tentatively making my way in, I could see the property was almost entirely full of all sorts of gadgets, lengths of wood, tools, inventions, musical instruments, and stacks of books. No furniture was visible as it was hidden by layers of smaller bric-a-brac that had been added over time. The last six steps up the stairs were visible, but the first six were obscured with even more bric-a-brac. There was nowhere to put your feet on the floor and so I teetered in to gain a full view of the task ahead while holding back from exclaiming any worries.

I tend to say "OK" a lot when homes are majorly full, like I am mentally cataloguing the scene. I like to think it is not giving away any concerns. Carefully heading through the lounge by holding onto bookcases either side for stability, I came to a smaller room I guessed to be a kitchen, but only as that was where it would typically be, as anything that would indicate its use, such as the hob or sink, was hidden under piles of random stuff.

Darren was brave at that first meeting. Subsequently, he was open to us taking a considerable amount of his former belongings out of the home for waste, recycling and charitable donation. We even used a skip, which we use much less frequently than people think, to clear enough waste to make the home accessible for focused sorting. The charity shop we work with allows us, with a quick call ahead, to drop off full carloads, and they were thrilled with the donations of guitars and books. On one occasion we found unwanted parts of a cello in the bath, and he permitted me to sell them for him. A grateful musician came to collect the parts from my home and the cash remains pinned to Darren's noticeboard years later.

I have learned over the years that this decision to let items go can never be taken for granted. An extreme example of this had arisen in the previous month. I had visited a family in Cornwall whose home was so full that the three adults living there barely had room for them to lie down to sleep. Their belongings were now pouring out into the garden. I had to start outside after time was allowed for baiting to have taken effect and dealt with an inevitable vermin issue. The woman I worked with was hoarding at an extreme level and the husband and son felt there was nothing they could do to reverse the tidal wave of stuff coming in. As a gentle introduction I suggested we bag up the outdoor items as they were now wet from the rain and deteriorating due to exposure and being possible rat homes. Black bags for the rubbish, white bags for the items that were to be kept. A photograph at the end of the session for social services showed a hundred sacks stacked outside. The decision made by the client, in the face of this tidal wave of stuff that was squeezing her out of her home? Ninety-five of the bags were white.

Back to Darren, who we came to see was not necessarily motivated by a liberating improvement in access and space, but instead fearful of what would happen if he did not participate in making his home habitable. He was currently living temporarily in the psychiatric wing of the local hospital. Now his medication was working, he did not wish to be there any longer but to be back at home. Making safe space at home was the ticket to him being permitted for discharge from the hospital. I did not even recognise the chaotic personality described in his care plan, as he attended reliably the regular visits to his house and was affable. There were only minor prickly moments where we had exceeded his quota of decisions for one day.

He attended with his assigned hospital worker whom we had to eventually distract with cleaning so that we could work with Darren directly ourselves. He needed a careful, calm approach and not the high-pitched shouts of "What on earth are you keeping that for?" and "Why have you got all this rubbish on your shelves?" he got from his support worker. We realised that we have a distinct approach, and we are highly experienced in working with vulnerable people and their belongings.

We suggested for Darren some short specific tasks of decluttering and made sure he had a chocolate biscuit break halfway through. We congratulated him on the progress he had made each time, and speedily walked him past the skip at the end of the session. This was not about clearance and throwing everything out. It was important that he kept belongings that meant something to him so they could be part of his recovery. But there are only so many decisions that can be made in a morning session, and so we had to build his trust and create established parameters on what could or could not go.

We were pleased that with a respectful and non-judgmental approach he made quick progress. The aim for all the agencies funding the project was that Darren would be able to return home once the home was functional, and that was achieved in under two months. That smile when he could sit in his armchair and have his gas fire reconnected for the first time in a decade was priceless. The great gain too was that he met my team member Rachel, and they established a working relationship that was to become a stable ongoing presence for Darren, long after his mental health support had been removed.

Unbelievably, in one session in his lounge, we located a complete, fully working upright piano that we did not know was there. It was a phenomenal discovery buried under the random debris of his more recent life. We carefully unearthed it, opened the lid and Darren sat at the piano and played a range of Beatles hits for us. This was such a special moment, as Darren had to this point been quiet and, though engaged, he was more of a passenger in the sorting process and gave away little of himself. Here we saw some of his true personality, and the areas of his life where he was exceptionally talented, and more than someone who has got in an extreme muddle in their home. Darren was emerging as a person from under the pile.

That whole home was entirely full and uninhabitable when we first met him, and so both the internal and physically represented journey remain significant. He is now not bringing in any other unwanted items and there is no spontaneous unregulated buying of items that could build up again, so that is helpful. But, through our work, we are acutely aware that these are rarely one-off clearing events that fix everything for good. With Darren, there is a great deal of worry and fear there and we are aware of continuing challenges, as we would now struggle to convince him to look at any new spaces. Now it is about baby steps and maintaining continuity as he sets the pace and focus. Like many of those who have been through a large decluttering project, there comes a point where it is difficult to go any further, no matter what the gain.

There are significant quality of life challenges that people are facing here in our local communities, and we find ourselves on the front line. Often, by the time I am asked by public agencies to evaluate what we can do, landlords have had to shut off boilers and gas fires if they cannot service them, or there are risks such as the heating appliances being completely obscured by boxed and loose belongings. Homes are often cold, dark and damp. They may not have a bed to sleep in as again it is blocked due to stockpiling, and throughways are treacherous as items have started to narrow the way and gather across the floor, making it uneven and slippery. The person may be unable to cook or wash as those facilities are not accessible. Plus, unventilated homes with hidden damp can be affecting their breathing or hiding structural issues that pose a direct risk to the client's physical wellbeing and potentially those of their neighbours.

There will be a lot at stake, but our involvement and the results rely completely on whether the householder wishes to participate. No matter what the carrot or stick is to propel change in the home, the anxious mind will find addressing the clutter more stressful than the risks presented by their hoard. We have started to use a checklist of key questions we ask public agencies or worried family members when they call, to give a clear guide on how significant the risks are. See the Appendix for the checklist.

We have been fortunate in being able to stay in Darren's life as an occasional support and this is a model of operating that we are trying to replicate with future projects. It is rare for us to be in that position, as often these big change projects finish when the funding agencies consider they have done their part. Too often we have not been able to secure an arrangement to create long-term sustainable improvement but have been brought in as a quick fix. Longer term involvement from a position of trust allows what I would consider normal levels of sorting. This is the route to engage the client more actively in managing their own home and so build their own self-sufficiency. However, if it is not the funding that runs out, it can be the client's will to engage that runs dry. So, we do not take any of our involvement for granted.

Securing basic home comforts for people is a true joy, as I am not sure we all realise how many people live in poor conditions behind closed doors. It is typical for us to see people sleeping in armchairs, with no washing facilities or a place to make a cup of tea. There is an abundance of stuff in homes but none of it is making their life any easier. In fact, it is conspiring to make life harder by creating trip hazards, blockages to normal facilities as well as draining financial resources. Trauma, psychological wars with depression and anxiety, bereavement, and a sense of being out of control can conspire and people feel like they are stuck. The state of the home is a powerful representation of what is going on inside.

Some four years after our first successful declutter with Darren, Rachel is going in for what we refer to as residual sorting, where items that had been previously put in boxes by us to gain footing on the floor are now sifted and looked through gradually, and more naturally. He will make her a cup of coffee, they listen to the same show on the radio, and create a real sense of familiarity about the process of cleaning and organising. Seeing the pride he has with the cups all washed and ready is a touchstone of our work. I recently visited with some storage during one of their sessions. It was arranged for Rachel's visit as Darren still finds meeting new people difficult, so we often time any trades work to be when we are there. I found them laughing at the top of the stairs wearing a range of vintage hats and folksy waistcoats from a long-forgotten wardrobe. That for me is what we do. Re-engaging, enjoying, and sharing tales with our stuff and maybe then even letting some of it go.

We tell him each time about how impressed we are with the small important steps he takes to tackling clothing and personal paperwork which we know he finds difficult to do due to the memories it brings up for him. He has revealed a lot to Rachel about his previous family life, the estrangement from his children, his battle with alcohol, and the psychotic episodes that led to his hospitalisation. Slowly she has seen some reconnection with his talents and hobbies such as playing the piano in public, some early stages of family reconciliation, and a sense of control over the narrative of his life. We have been with him on this four-year journey, showing how there is not a magic quick fix to such a significant stockpile. The real work is often painstaking but ultimately rewarding.

The transformation in Darren's life is a great example of the many real breakthroughs we see in our work. We see years of personal neglect peel back as we witness clients being able to return to their homes; at-risk tenancies being de-escalated and people feeling more secure in their homes; grandchildren being able to visit safe homes for the first time; clients being able to live in more than a tiny fraction of their home and enjoy interests again. What we do contributes in no small way to people being able to start to think about the future, connect with their former selves, maybe by playing the piano or at the very least, through enjoy sitting in their previously hidden armchair.

JANE
THE BATTLE WITH TRINKETS

Jane is an older lady living by herself on a council-owned estate in a home that is in a terrible state of disrepair. She and her husband bought the property under the Right to Buy scheme many years ago. Council tenants, under certain terms, had the option to purchase their house from the council. Over a decade later the homes around Jane still owned by the council have been modernised by the local authority and have solar panels, new PVC windows and inside will have been issued with new bathrooms and kitchens. However, Jane's home stands out as dilapidated, with fences that look like they may come down, with garden grass peeking over the top, and windows in danger of falling out. Inside, the kitchen cupboards are falling off the walls, furniture is broken, paper is peeling off the ceiling and the carpets are riddled with moths. It's a sad contrast to see on the street that their home stands out as neglected even though they would have previously had the personal finance to buy their own home from the council. It is not much of an advert for the benefits of home ownership.

We had been attending the property for a project funded by social services, as they found she was finding it difficult to move around downstairs due to the home being so full. I had a soft spot for Jane as she had a voice just like my grandmother's, with all the regional dialect and phrases I recognised from my childhood. She was also a friendly and open woman, with a whole heap of tragedy to deal with and now struggling with her physical health. She was, like many of our clients, living in a one-square-metre spot in her lounge and so all her medications, clothing, bedding and magazines surrounded her. It was clear she had not been upstairs in several years, since her son and husband had passed away. A stairlift was in place, but either due to the physical exertion required, or due to the grief, she had not been able to bring herself to go upstairs and see their rooms. Upstairs, two bedrooms, one large and one small, were full of the family's untouched belongings. It had been some eight years since they had died.

To compound the challenge to her physical space Jane had been seeking comfort and distraction for many years with a compulsive shopping habit. Friends had been taking her recent shopping bags upstairs, out of the way of the narrow throughway in her lounge, probably to keep her a bit safer. However, now nearly eighty carrier bags of brand-new gift toiletries, catalogue purchases, sparkly makeup and trinkets were on top of the dusty remnants of untouched folded clothes. Underneath the immoveable weight of a physical manifestation of prolonged grief, beds were broken in the middle, almost like a metaphor for Jane's current internal private emotional state.

Much like with Darren, she was amazingly easy-going in the first few months with the amount that had to come out from upstairs, and with agreed parameters she allowed us to just bring bags out without double-checking everything. Our first key challenge was to effectively box up and ignore the top layer of recent shopping so that we could review those items later in the year. The top layer is always recent additions, or "live" as we say, and so not for immediate sorting. The items surrounding the lounge armchairs are treated the same in that they are likely to be immediate everyday items placed carefully where clients want them. We start by carefully placing these perched "live" items in a box or on a tray so the client can be reassured that the phone/keys/sewing/TV magazine/purse/diary are to hand later when we have left, and they can reach out for those daily-used belongings. We can then in the session safely move to the lower layers.

Once the preparation was completed, we could start to go through the family clothing and ascertain what was reasonable enough to donate. It is at these times I am grateful for working with Rachel, as sorting through very old untouched clothing of those that have passed can be a bit sombre. We cheer ourselves up with some of the amazing fashion finds we regularly come across or when we locate an interesting piece of furniture. In these situations there are usually hundreds of individual items to sift through, so it is good to have someone to halve the time it takes to categorise and sort them. With this home, it was great to have one of us being able to keep going up and down the stairs with items to show Jane and ensure she was actively part of the process. She could have some of the joy of finding specific clothing that she was keen to see.

By actively engaging with their belongings, we offer the person a chance to review their home and reconnect with their belongings. If they are delayed decisions due to grief, then proactively facing those choices is best within a supportive and warm working relationship.

All this can be hard but taken carefully it can also be a good way to integrate those memories with the rolling forward of their current life, a vital stage of the grieving process. This also gave Jane an opportunity to speak openly with us about the circumstances of the passing of her husband and her son, what life was like before, and tales of the places they had been that were emblazoned on T-shirts we had brought to her to look at. For some clients it takes a few months before they open up about any loss, but for many it is immediate. If the client contacts the service directly then often I can find a long email detailing life events, health conditions and family dynamics and rarely any mention of the physical environment they wish to address. If it is a referral, then these have become two-hour allocations of my time as these details are revealed in the consultation visit. The confession of being overwhelmed brings with it its own package of personal stories that explain how their personal surroundings have become so cluttered. These intimacies can be vital as they bring a connection and trust that is important to our ongoing work. It means we can be sensitive to their unique context when a reference to a person or circumstance is raised by the client when sorting.

"That was Simon's favourite top."
"I made cakes for Catherine in those trays."
"I treated myself to those when I was in hospital."

There are all sorts of incidental statements that people make during these sessions, and we tune into them carefully. We can build up a wider, clearer picture of their circumstances through these, often passing, comments. Using those insights, we can be prepared for how poignant, or not, handling any specific category of belongings is potentially going to be for them.

In sharing their tales of loss within the setting of making decisions about current items in their hands, there is a glimmer of hope of an integration of their narrative so that in the present we can hold loss and optimism at the same time. It is poignant as we acknowledge the tragedy and sadness of events in the past, but then, at the same time, we are looking, in the present, at how we can improve their self-care and their basic comforts. While Jane told us the story of what happened when both her husband and son died within a year of each other, I suppose we hoped that she could make the link to how they would want her to be living now, what they would want for her. The presence of an item of theirs brought them 'into the room' so to speak, and maybe even generated some joyful memories and some glimmers of emerging from a suffocating grief.

There were some themes that we had to keep in mind in tackling the state of the upstairs and what was to be kept, as she was not able to get up there and so had to give us directions from her memory and her wishes. I took pictures regularly of the upstairs rooms and at each visit would show her what had been done so far, to get her opinion. Anything that had the son's favourite football team on it, or soft bears, had to be kept, and she requested we make up a chair in the corner with sentimental items as a memorial to him.

It became one of the most special tasks in my working life, furnishing that armchair with a soft blanket with Liverpool colours and wide-eyed bears.

This was a first phase of sorting for Jane, and the other sessions later in the year we called 'Christmas revisited' and involved looking through boxes of wrapped presents that had not been given years before, as well as this year's purchases. A moving moment was when we finally convinced Jane that she needed to come upstairs and see it all for herself. Though stoical and polite, she really struggled to step onto the stairlift, and it was clear to us that she had not been going upstairs to sleep in the lovely bed we sourced and made up for her. I looked round at the broken sofa and dirty duvet in her lounge and it broke my heart, as the provision of a new bed had been over a year ago. Grief is powerful and change is hard.

It is also a common misconception that when a space has been made or a bed prepared, that this new function or space will be embraced and used fully. There are usually all sorts of reasons why people have had to stop sleeping in their beds or staying in certain rooms, and the build-up of stuff to prevent access is often more incidental than the core reason, whether fully acknowledged or not.

Upstairs with Jane we started the proceedings of reviewing hundreds of pounds worth of shopping, such as thirty identical hand creams, fifty packaged fragrances, and anything from popular door-to-door catalogues such as cleaning products, tea towels and boxed ornaments. It became a curious mix of the joy of Christmas gifts and treats combined with clearly the concern we had at an unchecked shopping habit that was financially stretching Jane and funnelling her resources away from urgent home repairs. I could hear Rachel saying, "Ah this is lovely, who is it for?" from the next room where I was furiously trying to maximise any storage space under beds and deal with broken cupboards. I knew that about a third of the purchases they were looking through Jane would want to keep as gifts for herself. Call it intuition or experience with compulsive shopping but I know it is a challenge to part clients from those recently acquired items as they are not distant enough from the "mistake" of buying them. Jane would not consider any of it a mistake – in her eyes it is all here as it is going to be useful or even its presence crammed into drawers has a self-soothing effect.

Special offers at discount stores and door-to-door catalogues sales offer a wonderful sparkly world but the absurdity of commercialism is clear when you are stood (as standing room only) with an elderly person who is sat on a shredded sofa in a home that is clearly hanging together by a thread, surrounded by bags of unopened packaged gifts. There is a voice inside me for sure that is high-pitched, screechy and self-righteous saying, "Can't you see how frivolous hundreds of pounds of boxed gift toiletries are when your windows are about to fall out!" Yet treating someone like a naughty child is not helpful. Not on either side of the dynamic. Adult to adult, I remind myself, as I recollect a bit of Eric Berne from my degree studies. So, outwardly I offer a more measured chat, acknowledging their need to self-soothe while probing delicately for strategies to channel this spending towards urgently required savings.

Professional decluttering has impacted on my ability to enjoy Christmas indulgences, due to dealing with Christmas trinkets every month of the year in our work when we invariably unearth a hoard of Christmas decorations. Some people genuinely love the festive vibe and I have lost count of all the cards, advent calendars, decorations, baubles, tinsel, ornaments, free standing Santas and nativity scenes which we have had to box up and label for the loft. It is in fact a nice, satisfying organising task. But shopping at Christmas has now been ruined for me whenever I spy rows and rows of horribly familiar products in the shops that I have either frequently decluttered from clients' homes as they have been spurious acquisitions that they have come to regret, or they are still resolutely crammed into a dangerously full home forlornly emphasising just how sad consumerism can be. All this reinforces my view that most of what there is out there to buy we don't really need.

With clients like Jane, I think Christmas may have had a role to play in her coming to terms with her bereavement – the wrapped and bought gifts that had been waiting for years are heart-breaking evidence of that. We have previously, in other homes, removed wrapped Christmas gifts from lofts and the client has been in tears explaining how his family had all separated one Christmas many years ago. With his permission we have discreetly unwrapped the children's toys and put them in the donation bag. We have had clients who are paying up to one thousand pounds a year in storage fees for the festive memorabilia they will never put up and gifts they will unlikely ever give.

We are quite used to walking into a room and despite there being no comforts on show for the person, there is a multitude of free-standing glittery lamp posts, snowmen, and jolly reindeer peeking at us from behind doors. These adornments should inspire joy, but in a crammed home with curtains closed I look that plastic Father Christmas in the eye and ask him how he could allow this to happen. I realise he may be carrying a hundred-pound catalogue order in his red sack and is therefore silently complicit in the deterioration in my client's quality of life through all this festive-justified accumulation. In a true hierarchy of needs, in my mind, a comfortable bed should come way before having these glittering extras that may not even be brought out of the shopping bags to be enjoyed.

Over the course of a year, we are likely to find hundreds of expensive toiletries, much of which will have come to the end of its life after years of storage. Jane allowed me to donate just four of the lavender hand creams we found that day, but who knows how long they had been there and so these items may not even have been able to be sold by the charity. All this feels such a waste of money, manufacturing and plastic, or a sad, lost opportunity to give herself the treat of putting it on her hands or passing it to someone and seeing their gratitude. I stacked hundreds of pounds of trinkets and luxury toiletries into her bedroom cupboards that she had bought to feel special, and I know she will never use them. She is comforted in some way, I think, by simply knowing they are there.

It is not just Christmas; again and again we see this mismatch between an idealised sense of what the home should be like against day-to-day reality. We found around forty large boxes of expensive garden ornaments in the lounge of a home we were aiming to make fire safe for the local authority landlord. Suffice to say, the garden and much of the house was entirely inaccessible, yet the owner had continued to go out and purchase hundreds of pounds worth of garden adornments that will not see their way out of the box, potentially ever. I can feel annoyed and frustrated at the client for impoverishing themselves with both the spend and the resulting limiting of their living space. But there is also bafflement at how she carried on buying all this while it stopped her being able to put on the fire to stay warm in the winter, long after the garden grass had reached shoulder height outside.

But this sense of frustration is balanced by a huge dose of genuine relief and gratitude that this person has been able to let us put some items out for charitable donation and start to see some way around her home. We may be funded for two or three sessions, and the client will be grateful for some space, but we know there is so much more to be done, and chances are that the spending habits will not change like the waving of a magic wand. All we can hope for is that when faced with the reality of the cumulative effect of the shopping that they feel they have enough, feel grateful, or realise they have duplicates, and know where to put their hands on something. A stocktake and visually seeing the extent of the bounty more clearly may offer some security and reassurance that could then reduce the impulsive buying. We can but hope.

It is the juxtaposition of the lavishness of the purchases versus the chaotic state of the home that add a surprising element. The top-of-the-range steam cleaners bought by householders where there is no visible floor, with five other vacuum cleaners parked alongside. Rolls of expensive wallpaper where there is no prospect of access to the walls for many years, even with our limited funded support. "I am going to decorate that room," the client will say, and I will think, "We will be lucky to even get into that room." There is a jump ahead in their heads to a dream home, without a solid acknowledgement of the steps that must be taken to prepare the space to be ready for such special additions and finishing touches.

We have come to accept that our clients want a magic answer that will look to solve their problems rather than engage with the painstaking physical task of picking up items from the floor for several hours. I have seen more unopened bottles of bleach in a home that was deemed unhygienic to live in than on my local supermarket shelves. One item used for its purpose is better than fifty that are stored as if they will do something miraculous on their own, like the mops and buckets in the Sorcerer's Apprentice scene from *Fantasia*. I sympathise – I am sure I bought psychology books as a student that I thought would teach me by osmosis. However, it is only by engaging actively with our purchases that they become useful to us. Hence the need to unpack shopping bags and have a plan. Or, better still, have a plan before we shop.

We have seen recently purchased luxury bedding in a home where there was no operational bed, and instead the client has been sleeping on an old sofa for fifteen years. The client's diagnosis of post-traumatic stress disorder and obsessive-compulsive disorder meant that it was not going to be easy to get a bed up and running. We have shifted huge volumes of healthy-eating gadgets and exercise equipment in homes of those who cannot even access their kitchens or due to physical ailments find it hard to even move to another room. I would jump with joy at the thought of a first day that a goose-feathered duvet could be enjoyed by my client, and she would sleep between her bought Egyptian cotton sheets, but I am realistic that this may never happen. We know there is a logic there for the client, and a sense of trying, but all too often, at the time we arrive to assist, we are usually months away from the client being able to take advantage of using new items. And even then, that is only if they will stay the distance in the difficult act of sorting required first to see floor space.

A too-common sight for me is irreplaceable wonderful items propped up against a wall of unprocessed random mixed belongings and maybe rubbish blocking access to the floor, windows, doors and furniture. I will know shortly whether Jane gave her Christmas gifts to her remaining family this year.

LEAH
SIFTING THROUGH FINGERS

The challenge in our line of work is detecting when and where the pockets of resistance will be. Sometimes it is obvious, as in when I am sent to conduct a consultation for the local authority and the person will not let me across the threshold of their home, or the one time I returned after a jolly initial consultation and the client hid behind the sofa so as not to open the door to start the next session. Sometimes the manifestation of the fear of moving things about is obvious, but sometimes it can surprise us.

When I met Leah, like many of those whose homes have become very cluttered, she revealed a back story of acute tragedy, telling me how she had lost her twenty-year-old daughter suddenly some ten years previously. Leah was dressed in about four layers of clothes and a woollen hat, and she sat in the far corner of the room next to a shelf with ornaments that were all a dusty grey, in a sort of nest of papers and magazines. A cat was sleeping on an open ring binder. In the private sanctuary of her home the whole story came out within moments of me entering the door. A wave of personal tragedy in every detail crashed into the conversation, as we stood surrounded by papers all over the floor, laundry banked up on the sofa, and all sorts of household items on every surface.

A deluge of personal information and intimacies characterise many of my early conversations when there is pronounced chronic overwhelm in the home. Some clients even email me lengthy descriptions of their trials and tribulations without actually explaining what physically in their home they wanted to see changed. I am not sure that happens much in other jobs in the trade spectrum. But this uncontrolled wave of trauma is replicated in the sensory overload of belongings piled up wherever the eye wanders. I stood there that day with Leah, psychologically holding onto my personal rudder and physically teetering as there was nowhere to steady my hand while I balanced on top of an unsteady, slippery carpet of free newspapers, flyers and unopened post.

I was there to solve a practical problem for social services of making the property safe for Leah to live in, and reduce her chances of hospitalisation. This meant for us, gaining proper unencumbered throughways throughout the property, gathering up the treacherous floor covering of unprocessed mail for solid footing, and creating access to basic home comforts like a clear worktop space, somewhere to sit, and a bed for Leah to sleep in. But the early visit is rarely about that. Within minutes I see what we could do to create the change, a bit like in *The Lego Movie* where the Master Builder can see how all the component pieces scattered about can be brought together to make something new and cohesive.

However, the real challenge is the personal relationship, building trust and reassurance. I spent an hour having a tour of Leah's home. This type of tour is often the longest anyone has been in someone's home for many years. In Leah's home, each room was colder than the last, with untouched piles of belongings furnishing every space, and I was aware that I may have been the first pair of eyes seeing upstairs for a decade. I was soon able to feel that so much had happened to Leah to erode her faith in others over the years and this was always going to be challenging. The best I hoped for in that moment was to lower any defensiveness by reassuring her that we were not there to rob her of precious treasures in her home and that she would not lose control of what happened there.

These consultations and early sessions are a strange time when you can feel like the resistance to change is already weighing down your arms and feet in that home. The dance of being empathic in a world of trauma that feels to your client as if it happened just yesterday, is something to be negotiated carefully so that you can still stay focused and at least outwardly calm. I have felt desperate to escape that space and take some time to breathe, I think it's important to admit that. The hoarding programmes on television allow you to see terrible circumstances and then be part of the Hero's Journey towards change, but what if you had to see four hours of someone living in that dangerous, isolated, cold environment and then hear the voiceover say that this person was in the same circumstance three years later. That is not enthralling, it just feels sad.

The scattered and chaotic nature of Leah's home was combined with the fixed and immovable mindset of someone caught in the headlights of fear and atrophy. Even pulling back into professional mode can be seen by the client as rejection and cause even more defensive behaviour. It is all a minefield.

On the day of our first session, I made the introductions, and we smiled and said we were pleased to be there. I placed our basket of coloured bags, gloves, labels, pens and tape securely on top of the clothing that was on the sofa. I had brought in some small cardboard archive boxes to help contain the volume of paperwork scattered across the lounge and dining area. The first step was to gather up the papers lying across the floor space and in carrier bags dotted about and try to label broadly the dates the boxes may pertain to, and type of items within. A hesitant nod is given and Leah retreats to the corner of the sofa so she can view what we are doing and take comfort under her blanket. After half an hour we had a box for miscellaneous non-paper finds such as cameras, kitchen utensils, plates, hand sanitisers and books. We also had a box for photographs and certificates, and we had three boxes of paperwork dating back at least eight years. Nothing was being thrown away.

Then Leah started asking us to give her each piece of paper that was in our hand and would then start to stack these papers in a pile behind her like a jigsaw pillow that she was knitting back together, or a highly unusual filing system with a human suspension folder. She became agitated at the sight of items being moved and boxed and started to tell us off for touching her stuff. This was not the first time this has happened, and we tend to suggest stopping at that stage and finding a different task we can work on together. It was agreed that the bottom step on the stairs would be tackled with one of us sitting with her patiently as she processed each item to her satisfaction. For efficient, practical people such as Rachel and I this can mean sitting on our hands with great patience, as this would be deemed a five-minute task with a dustpan and a bin bag for most people.

No other visual memory sums up what type of assignment this was than Leah's way of handling the detritus on that stair tread that day. Some clients will let you fill a skip and not even look at it as it is taken away on the day. Yet some clients, as with Leah, take the small specks from the stairs that she has been walking on for years and sift them through their fingers like she is panning for gold. In their mind I think they consider there may be something vitally important amongst it, but only at the very point they are facing someone about to sweep it up and put it in the bin. We know that these stairs have been ignored, stepped on and treated without regard for years, but now, suddenly, anything on them is precious if it is about to leave the house. That sort of sift of tiny bits and pieces is time-consuming, energy draining and, for us, concerning. There is so much fear and worry, and experience has taught me that Leah is unlikely to see through more than a couple of sessions before she finds sorting her belongings too overwhelming, even with our best intentions. Plus, at this rate the twenty hours quoted to the funding agency will barely scratch the surface of all that is required to reintroduce key functions to the home.

Rarely do even trained mental health professionals have to sit in a cold hallway for hours seeing their clients relive their trauma and see so clearly how it is limiting their everyday living. The repeated cycle of restricted processing capacity, frustration and fear can be like a vortex dragging everyone down. This job is not for the faint-hearted either physically or emotionally.

Crossing the threshold into someone's safe space not only means any challenges are more acutely felt, but you unavoidably plunge into the world of another person, and there is a huge amount of tragedy and chaos out there. Unpacking old boxes can be opening Pandora's Box and for some clients, alas like with Leah, it will be too much, and they will not want to go any further – you just never know. We worked in the kitchen and found foodstuffs in the cupboards that were thirty years old that she would not let go of to allow for the storage of stockpiled recent shopping off the floor and out of the hallway.

Forty bags-for-life were in the hallway and these quality bags cannot be squashed up like their flimsy predecessors and will not be moved on by householders. We have had clients only able to use these bags once due to intrusive thoughts about contamination yet buy bags-for-life at a higher expense perhaps feeling that they are doing the right thing. Most of our clients forget to take their canvas bags or bags-for-life with them to the shops. But to do the right thing in their view they buy another while out and this ends up happening compulsively.

We discovered, on those stairs, that Leah was not ready for a decluttering project, with the fear of change deemed a larger risk by her than the obstructions to her practical life. It is a comforting burrow that people like Leah have created, using a familiar narrative for their lives and the very real physical wall of items. To us it might be seen as a horrible dark prison cage, but it is their comfort, no matter how illogical that seems. Careful coaxing is the only option and small shards of light are a start, no matter how tempting it is to tear the wall down. If you are reading this with family who have been affected by hoarding, you will know how difficult this is. You just want them to be free.

There is a balance between empathy and boundaries. We find we constantly need to balance the impulse to help people towards recovery with the temptation to dive in and hoist them over our shoulder superhero-style and whisk them off to safety. Who am I to rush into a burning building, grab them and run out to safety? Invariably, they do not see the building is on fire – they are comfortable, and their home is nice and toasty and not in peril. My rushing in will make matters confusing and it is unwelcome.

So, a sophisticated, unconscious dynamic discourse takes place in this very strange situation between potential client and declutterer. Both of us are there, in the moment, bashing it out in real time, moving in and out of the rougher waters of the background story and holding onto a more hopeful direction of travel. Positive gains can be articulated in terms of reclaiming basic home comforts or access to hobbies, and those act as beacons on the horizon. But sometimes people do not want to get into our rescue boat. Leah was metaphorically touching the rope that the boat was tied to perhaps out of curiosity, but that day we found that she would not have the confidence to leave the shallows.

ENID
LOST THINGS

Enid was perched on the single bed in the spare room. I was picking up clothing that had filled the floorspace and covered furniture, and placed it in one area for us to start reviewing. My aim was to clear the doors to the grand ornate wooden wardrobe that looked like it may have access to Narnia. The first challenge was to make polite conversation with Enid and perhaps give her a small task while I cleared clothing to reach the wardrobe. I often look like I am digging an escape route, so I prefer the client not to be just looking at me lugging clothes about.

Enid, a formidable lady in her seventies, is sat sorting through a small pile of old paperback books, deciding what to take to her new home. She was already living in the new place closer to family, and so these sessions were to make sure the house was ready to put on the market. I started to lift the clothing, and today it is elaborate dark coloured velvet dresses and velour tops. It is our common practice to start a room by gathering up as much that is across the floor or blocking cupboards and to put to one side perhaps in our clear sacks so we can start at the back and work forwards and examine existing storage early on.

Half the time, once I reach built-in cupboards, free-standing wardrobes, chests of drawers and dressers that have been inaccessible for a while, they are half-empty. If not half-empty, then they are full of artifacts that have not been seen for ages, if indeed they remember having those items at all. Even if I encounter a full cupboard and the client wishes to keep everything, it is always worth letting them revisit what is in there as part of the organising process and becoming reacquainted with their possessions. Enid was mildly interested in what was in these rooms, whereas I am always genuinely curious and treat it all like an adventure.

We find that the contents of seldom-seen cupboard interiors are a rich source of meaningful sorting, particularly if the items have not been in use for a long time. They may be completely mystifying to the client as to why they were ever there and so can be moved on quickly. It can be a real shortcut to filling our blue bags for charity. Occasionally the integrity of the contents may be compromised, with moths having eaten clothing or damp infusing bedding to such a degree that it will not be salvageable, and these are easy options for the recycling or waste sacks. While we can bring some joy with a surprise vintage find, usually we are looking at fashions that have long since passed their wearability, and sizes that are entirely unachievable. "Fetch me the blue bags," I will say, and we can then add to the hundreds of sacks of quality clothing we donate to charity each year.

With clothing no longer encumbering the opening of this large carved wardrobe, and with its key in the door, which is not always the case, the doors opened for the first time in a decade. At such moments, we come across items which may have been owned by a person who has long passed or may be the sort of antiquity not deemed as special by others. It may be that enough time has elapsed that the client is confident that they have all the memories and keepsakes they need of that person and so this is not required to add to the canon.

But sometimes there are unexpected finds. A revelation from a cupboard or wardrobe can trigger stories from the past and a moment to reflect. From merely sipping a cup of tea talking about neutral subjects, the reveal of a forgotten item can then take a client directly to a personal memory, as if it is a time-travelling device. It is powerful stuff. We are on standby as we open doors and drawers.

Enid's wardrobe was opened. It was dark inside, what with it being made of walnut, and so it was difficult to see inside. It is always an exciting and poignant moment, and perhaps a small part of me is steeling myself for something unpleasant to deal with. Sometimes there is an avalanche of more clothes. Once there was a dressmaker's dummy in a wardrobe with arms reaching out like something from a horror movie.

This wardrobe was mainly empty except that one third contained a large dark mass. A bulky black fur coat was hanging there. My mind began to whir with the best ways to store fur properly and which cover would be needed and so on and in that pause, I did not even ask any questions. Enid leaned forward from her place sat on the bed. "That is my late mother's coat," she said. I had not even touched the coat at this point, but my hand was raised ready to bring it out to show her, hoping it would stay intact. A long pause followed, as I thought we may have a moment of reflection of her mother and the memory of their relationship. She then added, "I always hated that bloody coat." Older people unleashing opinions long-buried is always a bit thrilling, as you sense there had been decades of keeping quiet on this matter. These tasks of seeing the belongings in front of them can reveal all sorts of feelings that can now safely surface without judgement. "Shall we...?" I start. "Bin it," Enid instructs, and I wrestle the "bloody coat" into a couple of bin bags like I am wrestling a bear but trying to do it with dignity. Exasperated at the effort but trying to exude subtlety so as not to offend.

I enjoy the honesty of such moments we have when spending several hours in someone's home digging out items they have not seen for a while, and the permission they have to at last resolve a delayed decision without judgment.

"What the hell have you kept these for?" a partner will say, or an adult to their mother or father.
"Where have these come from?"
"What the heck is in this box?"
"Why was this left here?"
"Oh, my goodness, how did this end up here?"
"Why have I kept all this?"
"I thought this was stolen!"

These are rhetorical questions clients ask themselves as relics emerge from under beds, cupboards and untouched spaces. Every working day, in the hundreds of micro-decisions that a client may make in a session, it matters how free they feel to make up their own mind and deal with the consequences. Whether it be an elastic band or their late mother's fur coat, there is what they feel now, how they felt then, and how they will feel in the future. It is poignant and I consider it freeing to be given the chance to resolve the matter. But it does require a certain amount of resilience and trust in one's own decision-making. Maybe even some forgiveness if they come to regret that decision in the future. Decisions are made with the information they have to hand at the time. There is no handbook that tells you what you should do with your late mother's coat. Each to their own.

It can be truly joyful to facilitate the finding of lost things. I reassure myself that this happens far more often than losing track of belongings after a decluttering session. We have found vastly more lost items than being the cause of anything being mislaid. If you have decluttered and have not inadvertently thrown something away that in retrospect was to be kept, either by accident, misunderstanding or the client changing their mind, then you have not yet done enough decluttering. I dislike it when it happens, but it happens so rarely, and on balance the process is more beneficial than risky. If I did not forgive myself, I would be unable to go forward with my job. Same with breakages. Super rare, but they do happen, as we handle a million items a year.

At nearly every session though, we find items the client thought was lost to them. We found an entire drumkit in a small flat underneath woolly jumpers and a huge supply of new toilet paper. The client did know it was there, but we were very surprised. We were able to reveal it, make it reachable and they were then able to sell it. So, hopefully, someone is playing those drums today without realising it was lost for so long – that is a nice thought.

We conducted several hours' clearing with Enid through an outbuilding, and most of it was considered rubbish or items too old to be salvaged. It transpired that her mother, who had lived in the same house for several years, had kept everything. We were now reaching spaces that the wider family had not yet tackled to clear in the early days of her passing. We had arranged a waste disposal company to come in and they were busy loading up black sacks. The project had been four sweaty hours of bringing out the contents and separating out into 'keep' and 'not keep'. The unwanted pile was substantial.

It was in the last ten minutes when it happened, when we were checking round the shelves by the sink, emptying the last few cupboards with signs of rodent activity, and the waste team were loading up the last bin bag. Rachel picked up a broken mug and it just had some random loose items in there, a watch strap on top, nothing seemingly that special. But this is us, and we are hardwired to check.

The cup was handed to Enid, who was sat in the sunshine on a garden bench watching proceedings. She was weary, and we were starting to flag from the physical exertion of lifting heavy boxes off shelves. We promised this would be the last thing we would ask her to look at. Yet, there, at the bottom of that mug, she discovered a gold necklace that had previously been owned by her mother and which she had thought had been stolen. It was actually a special necklace and, in this case, a treasured possession. It could have been overlooked in the viewing of hundreds of items, and we were pleased that it seemed to be the reward for letting lots of unwanted items go, that something should come back to her. But I was also pleased that there was, in my mind, some sort of resolution about her mother's memory and here was a positive keepsake to trade off the burden of the fur coat.

It is a strange vocation that can have you saying hello as newly-met strangers and minutes later you may be straight into the heart of intimacy and personal stories in a way that is difficult to replicate in other environments. Perhaps medical professionals have this also, as we link talking about our bodies with every aspect of our lives and personalities. Touching people's stuff in their home can instantly trigger these memories. Our stuff has stories.

Enid was surprised by some of the contents of her own home but in that there is a hope of a discovery and an association with the role that belonging/memory has in their current life or otherwise. What I mean is that by maybe laughing at the preposterous accumulation of unwanted items, and the deliberate but forgotten storage of these unknown bits and bobs, we start to question why we have these things in the first place and whether they help us. What are their place in relation to who we are now?

I often reflect on the bravery of many of our clients in the face of awful tragedy and loss in their lives. For some it floors them, and they feel as if each day they are reliving the visceral experience as if it has just happened. For some they can move on and process it differently. For example, I have worked with a few amputees and when I have opened the cupboards and there are all their shoes, I always think that this is going to be a difficult moment. We are going to remind them of a significant loss in their life with the simple raising up of a trainer. Yet, without exception, so far, they have all been good-humoured and have brightly said,

"Ah I do not need those anymore. Donate them all." I am not sure I could be so lighthearted about it, but there we are, some people are amazingly resilient and can handle loss, reminders of loss, and still part with those items of that chapter in their lives without considering it too much of an imposition. You can never presume.

Enid sold the house, took her small bag of keepsakes and a few boxes of clothing to her new home near to her family. I hope she enjoyed the reconnection with her belongings. She decided she did not need everything she had ever bought or been gifted to tell her who she was. We gain a sense of ourselves through a constant dialogue with our belongings. Our stuff can surprise us.

ANNE
THE LAND GRAB

We see so many different types of homes. One day it will be a visit to a terraced house, instantly identifiable as potentially falling into dilapidation perhaps due to self-neglect. The garden will be overgrown, maybe with a stern sign on the front door about no junk mail, and a pane in the front door window cracked. The lounge curtains are likely to be closed with the lining sun-bleached. There is often an unusable drive. Then other days I may be navigating narrow country lanes, slowing for deer, to find obscure locations where a large farmhouse with substantial outbuildings will be situated. Today was just that sort of day, as I was to meet Anne whose new Aga had just been fitted, the sofas were antiques, and all the glassware in the kitchen was crystal.

A question I ask in any home is, room by room, who or what has the largest percentage of material allocated and for what use? In some homes I have described already, the largest percentage is in inert items stacked up, with a mystery as to what or why they are there. The fight for space has been won by the anxiety about letting go of items long past their reasonable usefulness. The person living there is losing out as they cannot sleep in their own bed or access their interests. But the question for Anne was not freeing up limited space to be able to move around, as this was not a bedsit with more clothes than a local high street store, but instead how the twenty rooms were currently being occupied, as Anne was living in a tiny fraction of her expansive home.

Anne had called me as she just felt things were in a bit of a muddle and she wanted to set up another guest room. But it seemed to me that she was squeezing everything in her everyday life as incidental additions in a small number of rooms in the house and giving up all the best space for occasional guests. She showed me four lovely, spacious bedrooms that were to be or were all prepared for family and friends who visited once or twice a year, and not all at the same time. Then she showed me the tiny, dark, airless room that she planned to be her study and craft room. She saw my puzzled face and started explaining, maybe even justifying, the arrangement. I worried that I was seeing her own basic needs squarely being put last in the hierarchy of personal requirements in her home.

Anne was not downsizing; she was a vibrant and chatty sixty-five-year-old with plans and hobbies. She was active on local committees and was handling all the administration for part of the farm. She enjoyed entertaining and clearly loved her family coming to stay. I do understand the sentiment in her role as a mother and grandmother for the family to be able to stay in comfort. With this in mind, I had to tread carefully but wanted to champion her own needs for the remaining fifty weeks of the year when she lived there alone, without sounding like we should make her relatives stay in the barn.

This is often a difficult conversation to have with people, as it may be the first opportunity to put their own needs to the forefront in the arrangement of the family home after thirty years of serving others and tending to their needs.

As frequently as we see unregulated compulsive shopping, we see people living in spaces where they have actively restricted and marginalised their own needs in various ways. I had just arrived in Anne's home and so I was keen not to upset unspoken family dynamics or present myself as critical of their existing lovely set-up. But it happens more often that you would think, that clients with more space that most of us can imagine have started to live in diminishing amounts of room and have set aside the largest, lightest rooms and the best furniture for others. There is some sort of land-grab in a home that tips the balance from how a space can be used practically to make everyone's life easier to it instead being tricky to go about normal business.

I left Anne mulling over my radical proposal that the brightest room with the best views could be her office. I can be seen as a neutral person that views the client's needs as a priority and I capitalise on being able to ask questions seemingly out of curiosity, but which are perhaps questions no one else dares to ask, or as a very gentle challenge to the status quo. The use of their practical space reveals some interesting presumptions about the person and their connection to those that live there or visit. I find it easy to encourage people to enjoy their own homes more, especially when, as in this case, we are still going to make the sort of guest rooms with countryside views and gorgeous beds that I would personally pay for as a rural retreat. Anne's family are very fortunate.

Across a year, in many clients' homes I can be opening kitchen cupboards and only finding unnecessary items such as balls of wool where one personal interest has taken over, meaning that vital foodstuffs are not being kept properly. Everyone has been inconvenienced by such an expansive takeover of one part of life. One of the land grabs we see is the spread of uncompleted interests and activities by younger children. We have many clients for whom the takeover is the creative aftermath of family life. Where there may be a person or child on the autism spectrum or with attention-deficit/hyperactivity disorder it is even more pronounced, as tasks are started and left and then new activities started elsewhere every day, and the cumulative effect can look chaotic. We can reset things, but we rarely change habits here. Some clients will blame lack of storage or the right sort of storage, but the real question is what each space is being used for and is it in balance with all that daily life requires.

Many of these clients accept that if the expansion of activities does not change then they will require support to simply reset their home frequently. In these homes, full of day-to-day living overflow, we understand that the children, or a person with compulsive behaviours, are not consciously taking up all the space to squeeze others out. Our involvement here has always been to assist with the management of the home so that everyone can live safely and practically amongst five hundred balls of wool or several hundred drawings of Pokémon. It is so often found by us that in family homes where they are becoming full, the mother's bedroom is the place where everything is stored, and that is considered low priority, yet to us it is the first point of call. Place the oxygen mask on the parent first and then they can be instrumental in quickly addressing the rest of the home.

I have always adapted my living space to meet current needs. As a teenager I moved my room around to ready myself for a new chapter. Ahead of my A-level coursework I changed my desk around so I could access my typewriter comfortably, which gives my age away. Even today I will be moving furniture about to make the most of the natural light now that winter is approaching and making space for where I want the Christmas tree to go.

Adapting and amending the home to suit current needs feels as natural to me as breathing. The sifting and decluttering is just part of that to make space for those new opportunities. I have no hang-ups or worries about being flexible and changing things around. But I have realised in my work that there are so many people who find that difficult to do and perceive that rooms must stay fixed, belongings must stay put, even if they are not adding anything to their lives. Things are to stay exactly as they are, and they are not even sure why. The person must just work around the obstruction and cope, rather than saying, "Right, stuff, what are you doing for me?" or "What can this room offer me?"

When I was working in local government in my twenties, I decided, in my first week, to review in detail the piles of old paper files left by my predecessor, Greg. In my view most of it was not relevant and needed to be removed from the office to make space for meetings and more desk space. I started moving it all and booked recycling and shredding services. It was an open-plan office shared by people who had worked with Greg for some twenty years. I became aware that my colleagues were spying me with a look as if I had set alight to a pyre with their well-regarded retired colleague on top of it. I may have had the right to make the choices here, but now I needed not to look too gleeful at dismantling someone else's longstanding kingdom.

Anne did create her own open office in one of the larger, brighter rooms, but after we had organised the guest rooms first. This was a compromise that worked for her and allowed her to enjoy her home as well as being the best host. I now and again receive a little email with a photograph of some pictures she has put on the wall to make it her own.

I say to my clients that so much is out of our control in life, but what we do with our stuff is an area where we can exert some power and influence. We *are* able to make decisions, and so nothing is immovable, and boundaries can be shifted.

STEVE
HEAVILY ANCHORED

I was standing in the kitchen space, with Steve poised in the lounge area in his one room bedsit in which there was very little floorspace. Steve is dressed all in black, the curtains are drawn and every now and again he shouts out random words. He is correctly answering the quiz questions on a television show playing in the corner. Unopened cans and packets of food and drink, books, DVDs and paperwork were meticulously stacked, and clothing was neatly folded and piled on top of every piece of furniture. Pens are lined up meticulously on any flat surface. Apparently, there is a sofa in the middle of the room, but I had yet to see it. It was slow going, trying to maximise any storage I could to create more floor space, so we could move around safely. This is professional speak for trying to pack things more tightly inside drawers and cupboards on a temporary basis so that your feet can turn round to change direction when you are mid-way along the corridor of stacked belongings.

I came to a corner by the television, and it was like Indiana Jones entering the Well of Souls. Rather than thousands of hissing snakes crawling along the floor it was the equivalent in black leads, all tightly interwoven. Extensions cables were daisy chaining onto other extension cables in an unending mesh like something out of a fire officer's nightmare. The fire risks in homes are always of paramount importance to our work, whether a Home Fire Safety Visit has taken place or not. I have worked for the Fire Service and their training on real-life risks is difficult to forget.

We see dodgy-looking portable electric fires with loads of papers around them, electrical loading, like the pit of wires I have just identified, and the usual concerns of how a person would make a quick exit from the building without tripping over on the way out. We consider any emergency access the paramedics may require to homes. If you had to escape quickly from a fire in the night in the dark, would you be able to do it? I was rather overzealous in this explanation when using it to justify not having Lego on the floor between my young son's bed and his door. He does not leave anything on the floor anymore...

A few years ago, I saw the aftermath of a fire in a home that was full. The householder had left the home for just a few minutes to collect a package from the back of the house and she had left one tealight lit on her dining table surrounded by her crafting materials. Due to the overlap and access to other crispy paper fuel the flames had started to spread across the floor and up the walls before she had returned from her back porch. The house was detached, and the fire crew were there within fifteen minutes, but most of the home was affected. Thankfully, the householder was unhurt.

I visited her a few months later after all the insurance assessments had taken place. It was clear there had been substantial stockpiling in the home ahead of the fire. Even the direct impact the hoarding had clearly had on her safety was not enough to change her mindset of the link between herself and all her possessions. Though each room was, from an outsider's point of view, full of rubbish, she wanted all of it boxed to keep. There was no reflection that the sheer volume of stuff had nearly killed her, but instead she was just more traumatised and worried at the prospect of anything being taken away permanently. But, even if she chooses to forget, I remember vividly what one tealight can do if it is in close contact to combustible materials.

I do not tackle electricals even though we have seen a lot of electricals. I will try, if I can see an easy unplug and untangle, and we have certainly worked with clients to label up what is what. It is revealing that more than half of what is plugged in is not actually in use or is not connected to anything at the other end. I am writing this in 2022, during a challenging time for energy costs and concerns about heating. If you have a chance to check on a friend or a relative who may be trying to heat their home in a way that may harm them, or lighting their home with candles, or have several electrical gadgets plugged in, then do. Though they may think you are fussing, I am pretty sure we are going to see an outbreak of domestic fires this winter.

Back to Steve's place. Near the electrical snake pit, and near the neatly stacked piles of DVDs, we found six dusty portable tape players blocking access to the now almost visible sofa. I optimistically thought this would be an easy win, with five about to go out the door. But no. Steve was adamant he wanted to test them all and as they all worked, they were all to stay. Such decisions do not have any logic – he would never need more than two tape players and that was keeping one just in case the other broke. I wondered with Steve, like previous conversations about food, whether there was a compulsion to own items at any cost. He brought freebies into his bedsit, unwanted food from his place of work, items friends had given him, things he had salvaged, bargains that were about to go out of date (and had long since done so). There these items resided in his home untouched, unutilised, uneaten, unworn, unplayed, gathering dust. It was a dispiriting sight. I was also concerned about him trying to plug anything else in.

What is more frustrating is when the fixed hold that these possessions have on someone seems to override all other priorities in someone's life, even when it seems blindingly obvious to anyone around them that they could cut themselves some slack. That is the suffocating and drowning nature of hoarding tendencies. Once in the home, the sheer psychological effort in letting even rubbish and recycling go is palpable and does not bring out the best in people. Friction emerges, as they are worried and may not be able to articulate why, and we do not yet understand what the problem is. We have had clients sift through bin bags before we have put them out and this questions their trust in us and the process, and so threatens how far they will be able to go in the endeavour. Plus, if funded by social services there is an obligation for us to show tangible improvements in their safety, but we can see how incredibly slow-going it is likely to be, so it is a challenge.

Our weekly fare is extraordinary volumes of unworn clothing, crafting items that were never realised, kitchen gadgets that were bought to make life easier or healthier and are not used due to being too much fuss and no space on the worktop to have them out to use. I am just going to list a few: yogurt-making kits, soup makers, halogen ovens, blenders, fruit presses, mixers, and hundreds of 'How to make healthy meals' cookbooks.

The second most popular category of unused items is books, which many people find hard to sort as they tend to connect them with their perception of their interests and intellect. The charity shops are not even keen on old heavy reference books which may have been bought as gifts but are left unused for decades so that the information is long out of date. Novels are good to donate, if in good order, but the ones that have not been heavily leafed through can pose a challenge for clients who need to forgive themselves for not having got round to reading that book in all those years.

My world is now so skewed by what I do for a living. I recently worked in a home where we kept finding bundles of newspapers all tied up and I wondered how we were going to address this with the householder and see if he wanted to store them, read them all, or cut bits out of them. But when I mentioned the bundles, he said nonchalantly that they were just from when he used to have an open fire and they could all go. No attachment, just recycle. In those moments we are truly relieved.

In a typical year we donate about a thousand sacks of quality pre-loved items to charity and facilitate the extraction of about the same volume again for recycling and waste. That is a lot of square footage of homes being liberated. In some homes that is harder fought than in others, depending on how draining the client finds the process of deciding to let things go. Whether they can forgive their impetuous purchases or naive optimism that something would be worn, used or read really depends on where they are emotionally at this stage of their life. We can only create an environment where those decisions are supported; we cannot drag someone to that place. If they are not ready to let things go, they are not ready for our decluttering service. Though they may want the result, or at least agree with some of the challenges of staying in a dangerously full environment, they may not yet be ready for the steps that it will take to get there if they cannot let some of their stuff go.

For Steve there was little chance of him coming up for air in that bedsit without releasing himself from the weight of the burden of ownership he felt. There is no subconscious transference of an attitude of only holding onto things lightly by it being demonstrated by us in the session. For sure, we can sow the seeds, and offer a different perspective for consideration, as long as it is presented in a warm way with no obligation. A change in perception cannot be taught cognitively in a handful of hours. It takes time and trust. We of course hoped with Steve that by revealing the abundance in his home, he would feel grateful. We could give him confidence that he had enough provisions and therefore allow some things to not be his anymore. But he kept all those tape players and was quite angry with me that I would consider anything less as viable. Ownership can be an oppressive master.

When you enter a home, you can see the psychological walls as they are represented by actual walls of stuff in a blocked up and barricaded home. But it is easy to fall into the trap of thinking I alone have the optimism to tidy up and make it all better. So many people start professional organising and find their clients are not as grateful as they thought they would be once space is being made. The relationship with stuff is complex and so there is real danger in charging in with a vision and starting to move belongings without properly gauging the anxiety levels of the client.

My clients are generally nervous about the prospect of decluttering, and so I just set expectations that letting go is not going to be as bad as they thought it might be. Getting stuck in optimistically to sorting is part of the behaviour we want clients to copy and then display. But then if you go too far, too quickly, you can face shutdown and upset as people feel it's too much for them.

Post-Covid, to be in someone's home working directly with the householder for several hours at a time, is the sort of privilege usually only granted to family or close friends. We are not family or friends, but in that close working, in that personal space, it is hard not to be drawn in more than is typical in other settings. You are in someone's home, and you observe them popping their head out of the mire and see a bit of light but then quickly retreat and drag a heap of stuff to weigh down the exit. It is a hard watch.

The managing of the mismatch between the desired result for the client but potentially the unwillingness to do 'the necessary' to achieve it is one of the hardest tests for us in this line of work. They have taken the important step of contacting us and have agreed to a consultation, which in itself is brave. They may have stood with us and visualised what change would look like and have indicated what they wish to aim towards. But only when the work starts do we know if they are genuinely ready or still not at a stage where they can associate their behaviours with the items they have acquired.

Steve stayed as he was with his tape players and humoured me for a few months with my highfalutin ideas of a new direction for his home. In his heart though, he still preferred that everything stayed as it was.

PHYLLIS

HOLDING BACK

I have been fortunate to have assisted several people in their senior years to downsize from large homes on Dartmoor to one-bed apartments in Exeter. We have engaged antique dealers to value items, listed items for sale, and instructed charitable clearance services. I continue to be impressed by how practical and stoical many of the clients have been in handling a radical move in their eighties and nineties. We had a client recently whom we were unpacking in his new apartment and he, quite rightly, wanted to be involved. Rachel and I were moving his dining table into situ, from where the removals team had placed it, and he took the other end. These tables are always good quality solid wood, and it was heavy. We did it as a team and he stated proudly at the end, "See, I am not dead yet!" as if he was telling the wider world. He was nearly a hundred years old.

We went to visit Phyllis as she was 'rightsizing' as we now call it. Matching the type of home with the changing needs and requirements of that chapter of her life. This meant for Phyllis no stairs, an apartment near her family, no responsibilities for a large garden, and a restaurant on site should she not wish to cook. A key challenge for her was reducing her clothing. I knew there was a large built-in wardrobe in the new apartment, and I had been to see it so I could see what would be double hanging space, long drop and drawers. I also had the measurements from the sales plan. Each room in her four-bedroom house had built-in wardrobes, some of it double hanging, and it was all full of clothing. There were four chests of drawers that were not able to come with Phyllis to the new home, and they too had clothing stored in them. I did a quick calculation in my mind that we were talking a 75% reduction in the clothing able to be hung and stored in the new apartment.

We had a civilised cup of tea in fine china cups and then went upstairs to start the business of sorting. Choosing the lightest room, with a comfortable seat for Phyllis, I started to bring clothing in from the furthest wardrobe. The first comment Phyllis made was that she thought all her clothes were too good to let go to charity. I realised that this was going to be a stumbling block as we had just weeks before moving day and selling so many items would take time, and they would need to be stored.

Occasionally a block to letting items go is that clients over-anticipate their likely monetary value. The explosion in online selling websites and apps has of course made it easier to value, list and sell any unwanted items. We have a collection of contacts such as local auctioneers who will answer my late-night emails with photos of pictures and furniture that a client thinks may be valuable. Most of those items turn out to be of no interest to an auctioneer, but it is reassuring to know we are not depriving our clients of an unknown fortune.

We explain to clients that using a dress agency to sell clothing has to be considered carefully, as an item of clothing must be pristine or high-end, and in fashion, you find that the interpretation of 'vintage' is ever-moving. The sale price needs to justify packing it up for sale, taking to the post office, or taking it in to town, and parking. Dress agencies will take about a 50% commission on the sale price so it has to be worth waiting for it to sell and having a fraction of what you paid for it in return. Once this laborious process is outlined, it often becomes less appealing. There have only been a few occasions in my entire career when it has been worth it for the client. We are glad to support the pre-loved market in all its forms and I understand that people may wish to make some cash during a cost-of-living crisis. However, all-too often, the focus on selling can unnecessarily delay the decision to let something go. This sets back a larger gain, which is access to all the other amazing things in the home which have been hidden. This is effectively like free shopping, as it saves the cost of buying duplicates. In situations where people are considering moving for more space or buying storage the financial gains of simply letting go of stuff are clear.

Charities need our quality donations. The people buying from them are in need, the people they raise funds for are going to be the sort of groups disproportionally affected by any cost-of-living crisis. I advocate donating to charity for all sorts of reasons, but mainly as overall, it is the easiest way for my clients to make the sort of big steps that are going to make their life so much better. Often it is not worth worrying about making perhaps a few pounds back on what has been spent on clothing over a lifetime but to simply focus on moving home or gaining a whole room back.

There are some clients who are not able to simply ask, "Do I want this or not?" and they are also held back by "Can I gain some value back from this?" or "Is it too good for charity?" This second concern is of course something I find challenging to hear. Phyllis had no financial worries at all, sat in her large home having conversations about expensive holidays. However, she will only let the clothing with holes and tears go into the donation bag. Twenty nice cashmere jumpers were re-hung, but twenty that did not fit anymore had to be rolled and stored because they were considered too valuable to be given away.

We tend to support Hospiscare (hospiscare.co.uk) or Children's Hospice South West (chsw.org.uk), as we have built up a good relationship with these charities, and their local stores have capacity for all the donations we bring each week. So, when someone deliberately holds an item back from the charity bag even though they have no use for it themselves, in my mind, unfairly, it translates into purposely denying funds for the desperately poorly and the dying. I try my best persuasive line when this comes up, but often their attitude is solidly entrenched. I look carefully to locate minor faults in the clothing if it is going to help make the decision for the client to pop it in the blue charity bag.

I know there is more going on and there are plenty of reasons why people hold onto items even when they do not have a use for them anymore. I hope you have this sense from me by now that generally I am an understanding and sympathetic person. But in these instances, I do struggle to have a poker face when that "too good for charity" line comes out, as I hear "These people who shop in second-hand shops only deserve my tatty unsellable leftovers."

Though rationally I know that the person is not being cold or heartless, I also know that charities work tirelessly to raise funds and that to survive and thrive they must make a profit. Though we will be happy to donate clothing that may be for rag use only (so the charity will gain in the sale of the fabric recycling alone) the value of rag is very low, and so they rely on quality donations to keep the good work going and people shopping in their stores.

We have, under instruction, boxed up items for a car boot sale that we know from experience will never happen, especially when again the logistical hassle and cost is taken into consideration. It is dispiriting but we hope to return months later to have a tactful conversation about why the boxes are still there. We sense the difference between a delaying tactic and a genuine ambition to turn unwanted items into useful cash. But we do what the client wants us to do. Bagging things up for a friend or relative is laudable, and I filled three large sacks for Phyllis' family. But they were still there on moving day.

I personally shop from charity shops and can be found dressed head to toe in pre-loved bargains. In my youth I was a beneficiary of donations from my older cousins. The black bin liner of clothing that had been outgrown would arrive, and in 1990 I would find myself rummaging through and being excited to wearing some amazing 80s colours and fashions. Magenta leggings and royal blue jumper – yes please! There are plenty of photographs of me rocking that look. But more than that it was a way of being cared for. We were a single parent family with concerns about any spend, and so it was so lovely for others to pass on their unwanted items so that I could make use of them. It fundamentally shaped me as a person. I believe in moving things on for those who will be glad of them.

When working with Phyllis, I think we both knew that more could have been achieved with the space if I hadn't been archiving loads of clothes she did not wear anymore, but that had become her unmoveable position. She was also experiencing her own loss with the move out of the family home. Ideally, this type of process is conducted a year after they have moved and are happy in their new place, but that is not practical, so I do sympathise. We are not always in control of holding back, as our brain is processing all sorts of considerations. To be able to let belongings go often requires a grateful mindset that says, "Life has treated me well, I can send this item I bought at great cost/was gifted back out into the world to benefit someone else, without even anyone I know thanking me for it. Cheerio green cashmere cardigan." What a great world that would be.

KAREN
TRADING STORIES

Karen and I are having strong coffee together in her open-plan kitchen and the light is pouring in through the skylight. We are both women in our forties, so we talk about our children, and I admire her friendly dog and I mention the beauty of her recently fitted kitchen. The assignment for the day is the bedroom cupboards that have become too full, and which now have boxes waiting on the floor for some of their contents to go in, which in turn is encroaching on daily living. Karen is asking if I can give advice on some new storage. I am thinking, let's look through first and see if new storage is the answer.

My approach is always to empty out everything from the cupboards right to the back, perhaps out onto the beds. This is a useful strategy as not only do I see more clearly the size of the built-in storage, but the client sees everything, even the items put in there several years ago, come out of their hidden confines and viewed in a more neutral context. There is something useful about these belongings being free to be moved (and, subtly, halfway to the door) and reviewed in the clear light of day. It is also more positive to decide on what special items deserve their place in the storage, rather than to focus on what is going out the door.

It is clearly a surprise to many what is in their cupboards, and we have seen the full spectrum of reactions from bafflement to angst or joy. These 'just pop it in there' or 'archive' cupboards as we call them, can harbour all sorts of paraphernalia, from the sublime to the ridiculous. We have opened a bedroom cupboard expecting linen and found divorce papers. We quickly identified a new place for those to be stored, as it is my view that any paperwork, especially emotive stuff like court proceedings, should not be in the bedroom at all. You of course may have your own opinion on this.

Lofts are interesting for this reason, and not just due to the logistical challenges. Securing a proper ladder, dealing with insulation, dust, broken boxes, which parts are boarded, and potential vermin, are all other factors we must consider as well as what the client might face in terms of types of belongings coming out. Lofts are intriguing spaces, as the strategy for any delayed decision is often, "Oh, put it up in the loft" and so we can find family heirlooms right next to fancy dress and forgotten camping kit. The team are usually happy to let me proceed first, as I don my head torch like a pro and go up the ladder. In an early loft task, I nearly knocked Rachel out with a substantial, 5-kilo brass camel as it slipped out of my latex-gloved hand, through the hatch and landed near to where she was standing to receive boxes. If ever there was an insight to the strangeness of our work, the client did not even recall having the camel. Imagine the insurance claim narrative if that accident had brought about some serious harm with an unwanted, mystery animal ornament. I am sure this is just the sort of way I shall depart this world, but to prevent that fate for anyone else, I now wear outdoor gloves for these tasks.

The contents of Karen's cupboards were much like the lofts we see – every piece of outgrown clothing from the children, every certificate, schoolbook, art creation, project, discarded hobby and unused gift. Many clients that we see have found it hard to sift through their children's belongings as they grow, perhaps not being in the mindset to prioritise what is special and what is just the flotsam of life. Karen had found just about staying on top of the constant changes that children go through challenging enough and reflecting on chapters coming to an end was proving painful. She had recently separated from her husband and so a reassimilation of what those happier family times had meant was hard to confront. Karen had not decluttered her children's belongings for twelve years but between us we felt we could tackle it.

A topic that has been taboo but is now a little more openly discussed is how much of our stuff will our families be sorting when we have passed. Leaving them with everything to go through is not helpful as there will be a considerable volume of it, and they will not know what you thought was special. In *The Gentle Art of Swedish Death Cleaning* by Margareta Magnusson, she writes about the Swedish idea of döstädning, which urges readers to slowly begin decluttering, so your death is not such a burden for those you leave behind. It has started to sit comfortably alongside other Swedish trendy thoughts on home organisation and approaches to life, like hygge.

If you do not know what hygge is, think about the explosion in interest in large grey blankets and décor to make a home look like a cosy Swedish log cabin. Anything that makes you feel like you are still wrapped in a hug, that's hygge.

In recent downsizing projects with those in their eighties I have certainly seen the cumulative effect of when that task of sorting memories from the everyday collection of daily stuff is put off for a further forty years. There is a pressing concern for what they will leave for their family to deal with and yet by then the amount and range of sorting can become overwhelming. It can be enough to put people off moving to more practical accommodation and so limit their own wellbeing, all due to putting off a gradual sift. When family have moved away and friends are more seldom seen, and we are finding it harder to move about and have the energy for taking items to the recycling centre, this is the worst time to start processing thousands of items from your entire life. Plus, there is the stress of change in a move, and so much is going on in someone's head, that all I can advise here is to try and start the process now.

Time moves on and then it is not just your stuff, your children's stuff, but additionally that of maybe a parent or grandparent who has passed away. You may end up inheriting papers, photographs, books and furniture to have to add to your own sorting project. I am not being hard-hearted about this whole issue; keepsakes are super, and we definitely need them. However, I have already started slimming down my photographs to a handful of photobooks, and I have a set of big Really Useful Storage Company boxes in the loft with special items that can be brought down at the first signs of dementia or sentimentality. The issue for me with keepsakes is that they must be accessible, as when we need them they are the only thing we need, much like the Air Ambulance, and to be accessed they must be of a manageable volume – what I mean is that we need to reduce these down to just the really special things.

I think that the hard work in the consideration of what belongings mean as memories is what makes my before-and-after photos pretty much non-existent. The true transformation is what happens in someone's head, not the physical changes to their property. The conversations and facilitated decisions about how to shape the space as suits them and their needs is the key work. A result of this is that I am missing the time-lapse transformations so popular on Instagram, as the substantial work we do is in the dialogue with the client on ascertaining its place as either 'keep' or 'go'.

I am just as keen on those visual montages of muddle to as neat as a pin. I see the appeal of the television programmes where rooms are dramatically improved with the journey that has the householder crying with joy. I have experience of these immediate makeover programmes and know secretly there is likely to be a large gazebo in the garden out of shot, full of boxes that will not move for years. But that huge step cannot be denied, and it makes for an amazing 'after' shot. It is just not a vocation I recognise as my own.

In those instant-change programmes, the householder has been brave enough to allow cleaners to come in and stage it that items are removed in just a couple of days. This makes for far more dramatic TV than the slow, gradual, negotiated removal of unwanted belongings over a period of weeks, months or even years, which is far closer to my day-to-day experience. The grind of making hundreds of hard decisions about what is to stay and go or a delve deep into the recesses of the past is a massive challenge and cannot be neatly conveyed in a TV transformation format. The cupboards at Karen's went from overwhelming to manageable, but they did not make a great transformative photograph. But the emotional heavy lifting Karen had to do, with myself at her side, was considerable and that cannot be captured on camera.

I had brought a few nice quality boxes for keepsakes for Karen so that she knew once she had identified something as being special that it was then exclusively reserved, put in the box and was safe. Karen and I sat together in each of the bedrooms, and I tried to see where we had movement on items from the cupboards that did not make the cut for the special box. The maths and spelling books from primary school did not show the unique character of her children but were just examples of rote learning. It was hand-drawn pictures and stories where their creativity was evident that seemed more special. The clothing that had a tale was kept or in some cases photographed and donated, rather than keeping everything that had ever touched their skin.

The practical advantage of moving children's items on nearer the time of the items not being in play, is that you can recycle them back into the community for direct reuse as you often have contacts to hand in an interested network. I am glad to be part of a collection of friends where we do pass on outgrown clothes and shoes and offer first options on books, games and hobbies that are no longer being used. It is part of my core belief that it is good to move unwanted resources out to be made use of. Whether it is to go to charity for sale, or to your neighbours' children, or even using the internet to connect to community in-need groups for items to be collected, everyone gains. I sold my son's pram to pay for his buggy, his buggy for the trike, the trike for his balance bike, his balance bike for his first pedal bike. I am not naïve enough to think I can get much back for his bike for his first car, but it was a help at the time. Trading in nearer the time is easier, a money saver and everyone in the transaction benefits. Plus, I have seen the results of storing prams for fifteen years in the garage before they are examined, and they can be unfit for any future use.

When sat with Karen that day we had so many categories I was busy separating out, and one was technology. Headphones, old mobiles and gaming sets all in a big pile, some with their power cables, some without. Occasionally I would find an original box and we would cheer. When years have passed, such items have not only been massively superseded and so depreciated significantly, but also the sheer effort in finding the power cable and box to trade them in can be hardly worth it. This is not a 'How to' book, I keep saying that, but do sort regularly, and trade in your old phone for your new one, or the old games console for the new one. This also has the advantage of having that bit of tech back in circulation, saving maybe just a few special metals from being sent to landfill. That day with Karen, most went into electrical recycling, which was positive.

Once practical recycling and less emotional items are dealt with then there are stories to be told about the special memories, and for Karen this was about analysing which version of her story was authentic and truthful, or something she just remembered as a story. Karen was juggling a transitional state in her life, and memories were conjured up without a place they could be filed as part of an established narrative of her life, so we had that position of a remembered item but not knowing if it was a keepsake. But we made great progress that day by clearing easy wins of what we could see were not important anymore or broken, and void of any attachment.

Some of my clients have crystal-clear memories about where items were bought, who gifted them, and every specific detail. I do not have a good memory, but I have begun to realise that this can be a burden for my clients, as when they remember the story, they consider that it must be important, therefore it must be a valuable keepsake. But just because something is accurately recalled does not mean it is a crucial part of our story. Recalling the fine detail of an item can, on occasion, obscure the larger picture when it comes to where it fits in our flexible story of ourselves and so whether to let it go. I have had several clients who have listed in texts, emails, letters and over the phone about ten obscure items that they want to look for, but without any context about whether they are keepsakes – it is simply that they can remember those items. They may be key keepsakes, they may not.

Cupboards and lofts like Karen's will always offer those challenges of what is special and what is not, as we reveal the mundane and the unexpected right next to each other. We had a few "I am going to kill him!" in reference to her estranged husband who had stored random unsorted memorabilia. She meant it in good humour, but it was a significant moment, with permission to be honest and annoyed. Though I should add, she has not killed him but has signed the divorce papers. She now has working cupboards, has marked the end of a chapter with her children becoming teenagers with some lovely keepsakes in a special set of boxes. I genuinely hope she has now been able to start a new box of reminders of future happy memories in her next chapter.

OWNING

TAKING BACK CONTROL

I love the 1986 film *Labyrinth*. In one scene, the main character, Sarah, finds herself back in her bedroom as if the whole journey in the labyrinth has been a dream. She opens her door, and an elderly woman comes into her room, but when Sarah tries to remember the important quest she has been on the woman keeps handing her childhood soft toys and collections and weighing her down with them. Sarah tries to recall what she was doing before but the woman says, "Everything you've ever cared about is all right here. What's the matter my dear, don't you like your toys?" Then Sarah has an epiphany and says, "It's all junk!" then fights her way out to re-embark on her mission.

That scene is a cathartic watch and I cheer at the "It's all junk!" line and the determined way in which our hero climbs over it all to start the real-life business at hand. In this case of course, a fictional mission to save her stepbrother Toby from the clutches of Jareth the Goblin King. But, stay with me, she is climbing over the inanimate distractions to go and do something important.

I spend my days carefully navigating the curious paths that belongings have shaped in homes where stuff may have been given free rein to restrict ambitions, hopes, interests and identity. The stockpile can define the person as if the owner is owned. It is great for me to see a representation on the screen, even if in a fantasy film, of that power being completely reversed. But we all have invested and given significance to our belongings, so we know the hold they can have on us, whether it is a to a lesser or greater extent.

Decluttering can change people's lives, often bringing self-respect and hope that can replace inertia and uncertainty. We have seen great achievements when people who have experienced more trauma that I could ever imagine, work together with us to solve the challenge of the access to their home in a way that it becomes an intrinsic part of their recovery.

By sharing these stories, I hope this has achieved two things. First, that hoarding and living amongst too much stuff is not just something to be dismissed as eccentric behaviour. Its roots and causes are varied and complex, although often centred around grief and loss, and therefore our first instinct should be compassion and understanding.

The second point is that we can all acknowledge that we have a complicated relationship with stuff, be that clothes, gadgets, books, keepsakes, photos, foodstuffs or furniture. One person's 'collecting' is another person's 'hoarding', 'wisely stocking up' might just be over-buying. All these judgements and relationships are individual and can be puzzling. So, maybe it is time to have a conversation with yourself about your stuff and perhaps re-evaluate your relationship with it.

All of us could do with adopting a more conscious and considered approach to buying, using, keeping, and letting go of stuff, as the effects of this can be far-reaching. We have become increasingly aware of the impact this can have on the environment and the world's climate. But perhaps take some time to consider how you interact with stuff, to collecting, to wanting, to consuming, and your relationship with your family and friends' attitude to *their* stuff. These become concentric circles of stuff, all having an impact on our lives every day. It is good to own things, but we need to start to say when enough is enough.

The title of this book is *Being Owned*, hinting that all too often, instead of us owning our stuff, we are being owned by it, surely an unhealthy switch in the balance of power. We need to restore that relationship to one in which we are back in control, and not be captive to its vice-like grip. In considering our resources as holding hands with us in our aims and ambitions for our life we can take steps forward. We *can* change how we live our lives and our living spaces for the better, and not face walls at every turn.

Good luck!

JASMINE SLEIGH

APPENDIX |

Questionnaire for Agency Professionals seeking funded Professional Decluttering

When social services or housing teams require a professional decluttering service for their service user, certain information is essential for us to offer the best approach for each individual/family.

Specialist decluttering requires full participation and capacity, as it requires collaboration. It is about habit change and working towards sustainable outcomes.

Kindly complete the following questionnaire and acknowledge the next steps proposed. We estimate this will take no more than 5 minutes to complete.

- Has a Home Fire Safety Visit taken place at the property?

- Did the Home Fire Safety Visit trigger a safeguarding referral due to high levels of stockpiling, causing risk? (Level 7 of The Clutter Rating Scale).

- Is the home at Level 9 and so likely to require provisional/ part clearance?

- Is the home squalid or infested? Does a deep clean or part clearance need to be attended to first?

- Has the householder agreed they are ready to make changes and engage with a decluttering support service?

- Are there children at the property?

- Is there a Team Around the Child in place?

- Are there any concerns or signs of substance abuse in the household?

- Is there any information to be shared with regards to any professional working alone in the property with the householder or any persons of concerns within their close family/network (for example, Restraining Orders).

- Does the householder own their own home or live in social housing or private rental accommodation?

- Tenant: Has there been a visit from a housing officer, whereby the volume of belongings of chaotic layout is now impacting on the sustainability of their tenancy?

For example, gas and electric checks cannot take place, or is vital modernisation not feasible?

- Has a Housing Officer or Social Worker considered the volume of belongings or chaotic layout as now having a serious impact on the person's wellbeing. That their home environment is increasing their risk of hospitalisation? This could be increased major trip hazards, not being able to sleep in their own bed, or having clear and easy access to cooking facilities.

- Has an agency professional assessed the mental health of the householder and considered that to manage their home environment effectively and to stay living in their own home, that they require a specialist decluttering service?

- Does the householder have full decision-making capacity?

- If no, does the householder have a Power of Attorney in place?

- Has the householder had issues with hoarding behaviours previously? Is this a recurring issue?